Mountain Houses

Editorial Gustavo Gili, S.A.

08029 Barcelona   Rosselló, 87-89
Spain
Tel. (343) 322 81 61   Fax (343) 322 92 05

Mountain Houses

Introduction by Ramon M.ª Puig

Photographs by Mònica Roselló

GG

Dedication

To the memory of José Antonio Balcells,
who so loved the Vall d'Aran.

Acknowledgements

First of all, to the owners and architects of the houses published here, for their kindness and assistance with the research for the book and the taking of the photographs. But thanks, too, for the pact of mutual confidence which, no doubt tacitly, must have been established between them at some point in order for these works of architecture to exist in the form in which they do.

Evidently, thanks also to Mònica Roselló, for the highly professional quality of her work, uninhited and perfectionist at the same time, which has enabled us to see secret facets of the houses photographed.

Finally, thanks to the architects Lluís Maria Vidal and Paco Puyalto, incomparable guides on my investigations, for their advice and their companionship. And especially, as an expression of my admiration for their determination to be men of the Pyrinees.

Translation: Graham Thomson

© Editorial Gustavo Gili, S.A., Barcelona, 1991

ISBN: 84-252-1550-1
Depósito legal: B. 26.124-1991
Printed in Spain by Grafos, S.A. - Barcelona

Index

Introduction

The Pyrinean house

There is a vision of the Pyrenees as a barrier, a vision fostered both by the autarchic spirit which dominated life in Spain for so long, an by and efficient and radical French centralism. This idea finds its counterweight in a conception of the Pyrenees as a bridge, as the bonding agent uniting peoples and cultures, as the cradle of "Pau i Treva" -peace and truce - (Toluges), as the redoubt of independence (Montsegur), as the focal point for the diffusion of civilisation (Cuixa, Roda, Ripoll)...

Both of these interpretations have their moments and areas of truth, given that the Pyrenees are so extensive, and their history so wide and complex. As complex as is the nature of one of the products of that history, their architecture.

Pyrinean architecture ought not to be considered as a unitary phenomenon, but rather as a diversity of architectures, with the common characteristic of the predominance of potency over richness. Beginning with a certain way of building which we call Romanesque, that rooted itself so strongly as almost to have come to be regarded as the national style, up to, and above all, a rural architecture which, with an extensive range of regional variants, constitutes a heritage of note, composed in particular of houses and constructions relating to the labour of the fields: barns, cottages, pens for livestock...

Whether the Pyrenees are a barrier or not, what is true is that the isolation intrinsic to a difficult terrain, distant from the seats of power, preserved this architectural legacy almost intact up until the nineteen fifties. If we leave aside totally atypical phenomena such as Lourdes and Andorra, only the occasional thermal spa and a few peaceful resorts in which to spend the summer intervene in a minimal, almost respectful manner in the rural landscape and its towns and villages.

Until the spectacular introduction of skiing in the sixties and seventies, and property development on a massive scale in the eighties, it had seemed as if the Pyrenees were to be spared the visual contamination and the degradation of the landscape which has affected our coasts for years now.

To build now in the mountains ought to entail the commitment not to contribute to this degradation. Here we have descriptions of a number of constructions which illustrate different ways of shouldering this commitment: private houses, contemporary and newly-built from the foundations up.

The analysis of the traditional house would involve us in a much more extended process of reasoning. Rather than study the region's popular, vernacular architecture, already covered by numerous authors, we are interested in looking at how the problems of building in the mountains are resolved by means of a reflexive and critical act, that is to say, by means of a project, and not simply, as has been and is still done, in a spontaneous manner.

Nor do we intend here to tackle the question of refurbishment schemes, which pose a very specific problem; schemes which are prone to occasional diversions of a folkloric nature, yet nonetheless offer examples of work of the highest quality, such as José Antonio Balcell's scheme for his own house in Gessa (Vall d'Aran), or Miguel Milá's house in Sant Martí d'Arbó (La Cerdanya). Although existing walls have been incorporated into some of the constructions presented here, the transformations effected by the project are so sweeping that, rather than refurbishments, it would be more accurate to consider them as being new constructions.

In almost all of the houses included here. the priority accorded to problems ot siting and the relationship with the context is due to the fact that, while such questions are important in all architecture, in the case of mountain architecture they are surely all the more fundamental. This might constitute the ground for a differential discourse on the private house in the mountains. The programmatic features and the internal organisation of these houses, evidently fairly basic - and in some of the projects shown here, the principal architectural quality - are nevertheles generally similar to those of family dwellings in other locations. While the space needed for storing skis and that for an outboard motor are not the same, family life by the sea and in the mountains, particularly with regard to the enjoyment of lesure, is essentially very little different. Factors of climate are undoubtedly more important, but nowadays these are usually resolved by technology rather than typology.

Place and tradition

While construction followed the same slow rhythm as the growth of the vegetation, the traditional Pyrinean house posed no formal or stylistic problems. The typologies vere accepted unquestioningly, and all the builder had to do was follow them. The emergence of the second home at the beginning of the century, with the arrival of the first summer residents, brought no problems, either. The single stylistic innovation, perhaps, was the change from the traditional model to the imitation of the Swiss chalet, an ideal that was pursued in a thousand and one variations, which most of the time had nothing Swiss about them.

The present reality of the Pyrinees, however, with the acelerated rate at which the shift from the primary to the tertiary sector is taking place, is too complex and changing too quickly for new building needs to be met simply by following traditional patterns.

The sports complex, the hotel, the service building, the apartment block or the new farm installations forcibly impose a typological change. Yet even with regard to house-building, thanks to the move from what were once almost exclusively rural dwellings to second homes, and above all to the rapidity of their proliferation, it would seem that the traditional approach is being called more and more into question.

This might be the case with regard to technological and construction considerations, but the way in which the traditional architecture has dealt with the problem of the site and resolved the formal issues continues to prove highly instructive. Each and every one of the villages, ''bordes'', hermitages, any human settlement rooted in the past, constitutes, in the Pyrinean regions, a perfect object lesson in how architecture can make the most of topgraphical, climatological and contextual factors. There are few settings where place conditions architecture as much as it does in the mountains.

The influence of place has to be understood both in terms of the weight of the context (whether it be the rural town or open countryside), and of the way the construction is set down in the landscape; in other words, how it is involved with the territory. The building traditions of the Pyrinees have resolved both questions in exemplary fashion. The way an Aranese village nestles on the gentle slope of the hillside, or a village in the upper Cinca or Cardós shelters in a bend of the river, or a village in the Pallars perches on top of a crag, corresponds to the wisdom of the reading of the place, its conditions and advantages. A reading which may or may not be conscious, but is the legacy, the fruit of tradition. That is to say, a reading which is at the same time a culture.

Equally, the way the buildings, in following certain typological patterns, have been grouped according to factors of scale, colour and volumetry, apart from reflecting the mountain village's sense of formal harmony, which affects us so deeply, is also the manifestation of a wise law governing the slow growth of the village. Conditions, and a law, which are facit, and no doubt unconsciously complied with –except where questions of property rights are involved– yet effective over the course of generations.

Beyond the archetype

The ideal picture people usually have of the houe in the mountains is determined more by symbolic aspirations, qualitative demands and formal conventions than by primary needs. This does not mean that systems of construction or functional imperatives do not count, but simply that they do not play a definitive part in the creation of the image. The idea of a refuge, the sensation of rural simplicity, the desire for solitude and other similar emotions are the sources of the ideal of the house in the mountains. Their power of connotation has enough synthetic potential to call into being an archetypal image above and beyond the actual variations determined by the variety of different functional requisites and construction solutions.

In recent years the various regional architectures have become the almost obligatory model for new building, adding the goal of identifying with tradition to the series of factors noted above. Yet even so, beyond all the typological diverity, there still exists an archetypal image of the mountain house: an isolated dwelling, steeply sloping eaves, wood, stone, slate... the Swiss chalet.

As a model, the Swis chalet is an entelechy. It includes the little timber cabin, the grandiose houses of the Bernese Oberland, and the variegated species of the 'colour supplement'' home. But when it comes to planning a new house in the mountains, it can be difficult to avoid the predicating of an archetypal image. The pursuit of this ideal has given rise to ingenuous and at times charming approximations to the paradigm, above all during the sixties, but also, as a consequence of the subsequent building boom, to the proliferation of banal, if not absurb, copies. Yet it is nonetheles true that it is possible to arrive at eminently sensible results without having to renounce these preconceptions. It is even possible, through the use of a variety of means, such as the manipulation of the typological elements, the unconventional use of traditional materials, experimentation with construction techniques, and so on, to come up with a scheme which is architectonically exemplary, that transcends the conventional image and manages to surpass, in one way or another, the archetype itself.

The Llum house in Planoles by the architect Jordi Llorens; the little refuge known as "El Pajar", "the hay loft", in Canfranc, by Miguel Fisac; the Gallego house, in Planés, again by Jordi Llorens; the Collderam house in Casarilh, by Carlos Llobet, are all examples of work that illustrates this possibility perfectly.

Other voices, other environments

The architectural references of the Pyrinean house are not always exclusively mountainous in origin. There are others, distinct from both traditional architecture and the Swiss chalet, whcih, while much less significant in terms of numbers, are by no

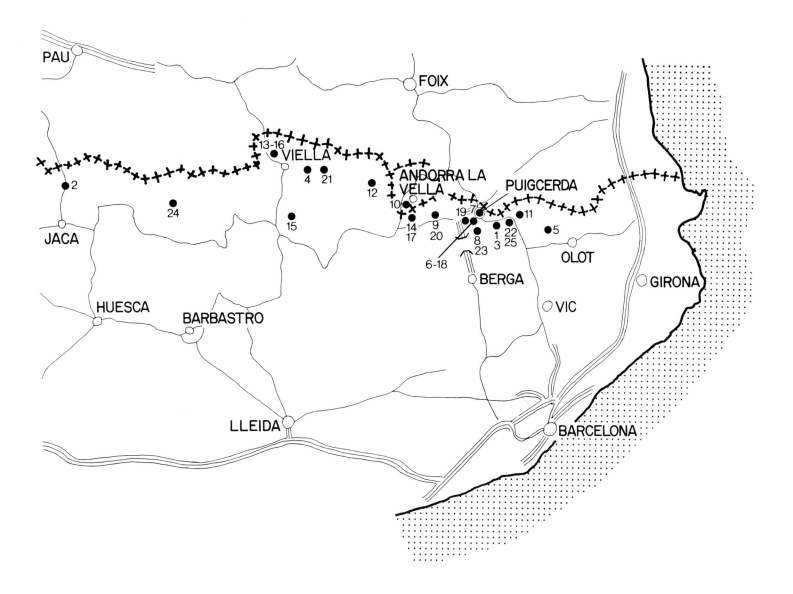

1 Llum house
2 El Pajar
3 Gallego house
4 Collderam house
5 Private house
6 Valls i Taberner house
7 Private house
8 Ajenjo house
9 Robert house
10 Curtis house
11 Cal Nap
12 Juvany house
13 Borda d'en Roy

14 Ca l'Agustí
15 El Paller
16 Folgosa house
17 Font house
18 Private house
19 Rius Fina house
20 Sanmartí house
21 Heredero house
22 Martí Campanyà house
23 Mateu Martínez house
24 Mairal Ceresuela house
25 Xampeny house

means less interesting. Such houses are the results of the influence of other cultures from outside the local context. There is, indeed, a whole repertoire which ranges from Catalan "noucentisme" through to rationalism and its derivatives, by way of the American prairie homestead, transplanted to the mountains scarcely unaltered save for the cosmetic addition of slate roofs.

In most cases these are not spontaneous interventions but constructions based on an architectural project, and generally located in residential developments outside existing towns or villages, which have grown up into autonomous entities free of any preexisting imperatives.

An architecture intimately bound up with the origins of the summer holiday, when the holiday had not yet become a mass phenomenon, which reproduces many of the features of the Mediterranean villa or the detached house in the garden suburbs of the big city, constructed by means of simple operations of formal speculation, usually the work of cultured architects. Extreme examples of this –not included in the present volume on account of their age– might be the Riviere house, near Puigcerdà, by Raimon Durán Reynals, and the Elías house number 4, by Josep Maria Sostres, in Bellver de Cerdanya: the first as a direct transposition of the grand villa, and the second following the general lines of Nordic organicism.

Amongst the houses featured here, however, the house by José Antonio Coderch in Camprodon; the Valls-Taberner house by Francisco Ribas and José Luis Cia and the house by Antonio Bonet Castellana, both near Puigcerdà; the Ajenjo house near Alp by Pere Llimona and Javier Ruiz Vallés; the Robert house near Prullans, by Gabriel Robert, and the Curtis house in Aubinyà (Andorra) by Estudio MAD, all display, in their different ways, a diversity of origins and intentions, and are clear examples of this architecture of quality in the mountains, although they are not properly speaking mountain architecture.

Contexts

As we have already seen, the siting of the house is a determining fator in mountain architecture. Of the complex relationships between house and place we can characterise at least three clearly defined types of situation.

The first is where the new house is designed to occupy a site in the thoroughly consolidated nucleus of a rural town or village, with clear typological constants.

The second situation is that encountered by a boundary site neither fully inside the nucleus nor wholly disconnected from it. What is often referred to as "the edge of the village", and which we might describe as a situation of extending the boundary.

The third applies to an intervention totally outside any kind of urban context, either a traditional village or a new residential or service development. Where, in other words, the project has to confront the isolation of the site.

In the first situation, the most rational approach in the majority of cases is to adapt to the typological standards imposed by the surroundings, with regard to scale, volumetry and colour. The Cirici house in Queralbs and the "Borda d'en Roy" in Arrós, both by the architect Cristian Cirici, the Juvany house by Joan Rodón, in Areu, the "Ca l'Agusti" house in Arcavell by Xavier Güell, and the "El Paller" house by the architect Guillem Sáez, in Barruera, have all, with some minor differences, been conceived according to this criterion.

In the second situation, the conservation of scale is still of importance, but the form, in view of the much lower concentration of existing constructions, will be less conditioned by its surroundings, and will enjoy much greater freedom. The same applies to colour. At the limits of the urban context, then, there is the opportunity of enjoying at least one or two degrees of freedom more than in the heart of the built context... Good examples of this are the Folgosa house in Arrós by Aguilar, Albors, Canosa, the Font house in Arcavell by Miquel Espinet and Antoni Ubach, the house in Guils de Cerdanya by Francisco Ribas and the Rius house in Bellver de Cerdanya by the architect Francesc Rius.

Finally, in the third situation, the new building has total architectonic autonomy with respect to other architectures. The only dialogue is that established between the new formal presence of the building and the formal structure of the place. Here the architecture is confronted with a natural context, which may be benign or terrible, gentle or dominating, even neutral, but never mute. It needs to be deciphered, and the architectural response, on the basis of this reading, might be anything from camouflage to total confrontation, from a whisper to a roar, with all of the possibilities in between. The house in Canfranc mentioned earlier, by Miguel Fisac, was designed, in its day, to confront this problem as an affirmation in the face of the geological rotundity of its setting, but the subsequent construction of blocks of apartments round about it has transformed the landscape to such an extent that the house's original meaning has been almost lost. Something similar has happened, to a lesser extent, with the Sanmartí house in Prullans by the architect Jaume Sanmartí, and the Heredero house in Tredós by Martorell, Bohigas, Mackay (MBM), although both these houses still retain a certain autonomy. The Mateu Martínez house in Tartera, also by Jaume Sanmartí, is part of a residential development, although because of its position on the edge of the development its true value, as orginally conceived, derives from its relationship with the landscape behind it. By contrast, the Mairal house in Laspuña by the architect Paco Puyalto and the two houses by Sostre in Ventolà, the Martí Campanyà house and the Xampeny house, clearly address themselves to the dialogue with the landscape, although in the two Sostre houses there is no escaping the relationship they establish between themselves.

To sum up, the relationship between architecture and its setting poses, in every instance, a completely open problematic, which in the case of the mountain environment is clearly apparent. Between the whisper which accompanies the integration of a house into a small town or village, and the potential roar of a new construction in the solitude of nature, there are a thousand possible voices of every kind.

Ramon M.ª Puig, architect

Llum house

Jordi Llorens, architect
Planoles, Girona, 1967-1968

The house was planned to occuppy a site with an unfavourable location and a difference in level of 2.5 metres below the street giving access. At the same time, the best views and the direct sunlight were to be found in the direction of this street. For these reasons it proved far from easy to obtain privacy without sacrificing sunshine and views.

These characteristics of the plot suggested the raising of the ground floor of the house up to street level, making use of some of the resulting underfloor space for garage and services.

The construction set out to create a house of the high mountains without resorting to the conventional Alpine chalet or the pseudo-typical typology. Nevertheless, the materials used are hose traditional to the region, although the layout of the house is somewhat unusual.

The clear, definite programme set out by the client has been satisfied in the minimum possible space.

Plan, elevations and views of the exterior

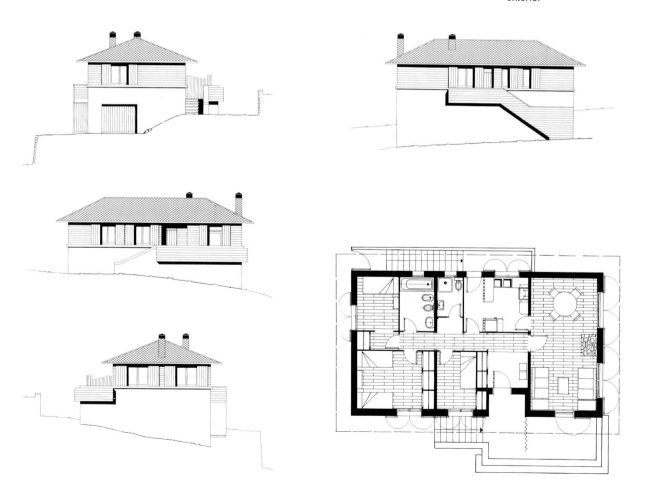

12

13

Various details of the exteror and
the access

El Pajar

Miguel Fisac, architect
Canfranc, Huesca, 1959

The programme established for this private house in Canfranc was extremely simple.

In the frist place, the aim was to produce an architecture in complete harmony with the beautiful and dramatic Pyrinean landscape in which the house is sited. Secondly, to construct a solid, economical and very simple house which would not require a specialised workforce.

The procedure adopted for these purposes was to construct wails of blocks of local stone, using pine trunks sunk into the stone to form the roof structure for ground and first floors, with a "windmill" layout of straps running from wall to wall as the basis of the slopes of the single and double pitched roofs. The tongue and groove jointed fllorboards on both floors, the planking overlapped against the pitch of the roof, and the covering of stone flags are all in keeping with local building tradition, as are the unsquared planks on the facades and on the vertical joint of the outer walls.

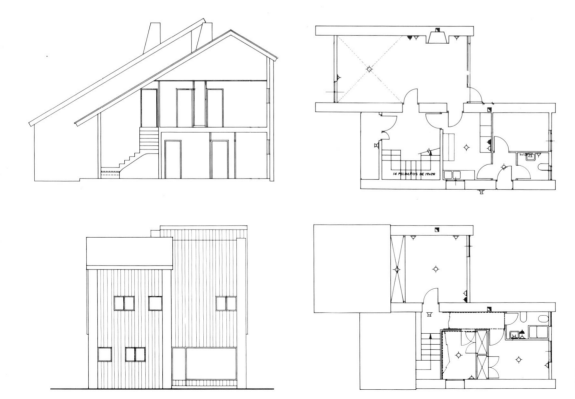

Plans, elevation, section and view of the exterior

Various partial views of the exterior

Details of the door and the wood
cladding

22

Gallego house

Jordi Llorens, architect
Planés, Planoles, Girona, 1970-1971

The site for which this single-storey house was designed was ideal, with excellent exposure to the sun, fine views and favourable gradient and access.

In the interior, the living room is separated from the entrance hall, corridor and distribution space for the bedrooms by a long, curtained sheet of glass which makes it possible to unite or segregate the different rooms.

The gentle changes in level inside the house reflect the topography of the terrain, which is also reflected in the pitched roof.

In keeping with the wishes of the client, special importance was given to the use of easily maintained materials, such as stone for the outer walls, exposed concrete for socles and roof vaults, aluminium window shutters and a zinc roof, designed to avoid the problems presented by the traditional slate roof in locations exposed to the wind, as is the case with this house.

Plan, elevations, section and views of the exterior

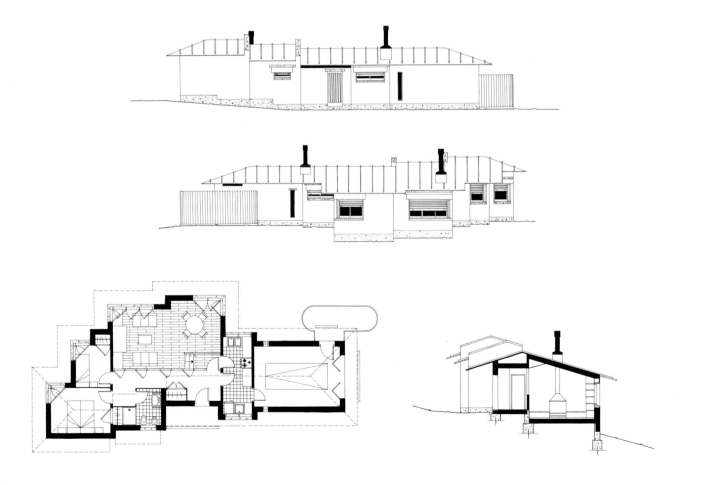

Various views and details of the
exterior and interior

Collderam house

Carles Llobet Roviras, architect
Casarilh, Vall d'Aran, Lleida, 1978

In Arán, the ordinary house is quite different architecturally from the "borda" or cottage.

The house is rendered, its roof has projecting fire barriers which are moulded and tiled, as well as being overlaid with such secondary elements as skylights and chimneys. the facades often have cornises and pilasters in the form of crosses and trefoils which highlight the rendering.

While the "market" tends to opt for the imitation of the "borda", perhaps with the intention of giving city-dwellers an environment even further removed from their habitual surroundings, the majority of my houses have set out to emulate the ordinary Aranese home.

This building, however, is based on the typology of the "borda", from which it borrows the greater part of its concepts: extremely simple volumes, openings in the walls as an alternative to an excessive number of skylights, and double-height spaces which give the interior of the house a sense of the volumetry as a whole.

Plans, elevation, section and view of the exterior

Various views and details of the
interior

Private house

José Antonio Coderch, architect
Camprodon, Girona, 1957

In order to adapt to the building traditions of the region, José Antonio Coderch has used the same organisational scheme, in the from of a T, as in previous projects, the most immediate source being the Ugalde house. The natural stone, which looks as if it were unmortered, gives the house a sturdiness of texture and thickness of wall which is counterpointed by the lightness of the sliding partitions of the white window shutters and the reflections from the pool by the east facade.

The reference to the Ugalde house's L-shaped space with its swimming pool and flat roof is resolved here with a similar area, although the roof here has Italian tiles which blend into the context of the surrounding mountains.

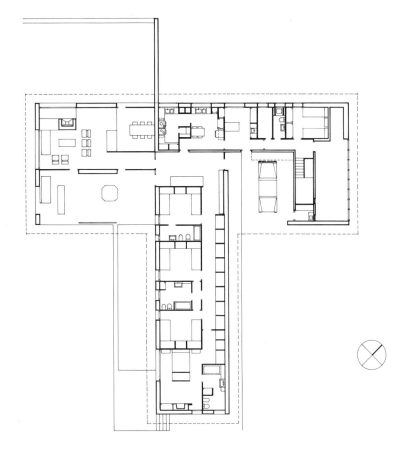

Plan and view of the exterior

Various views and details of the
exterior

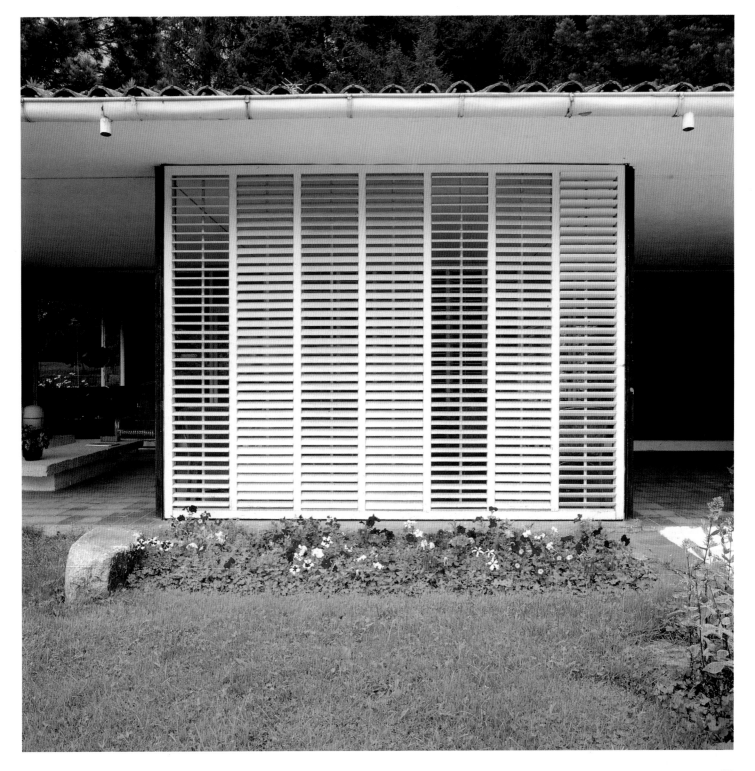

Various views of the interior and the
portico

Valls i Taberner house

Francisco Ribas, José Luis Cía, architects
Guils de Cerdanya, Girona, 1960-1961

This private house has been built on an 18,000 m² plot in the Golf district of Cerdanya. In this area, most of the constructions are large private houses dating from the 1940s and 50s, characteristic of more urban settings.

The building is composed of two volumes, one of which is the house proper, the other being garages, connected by a portico.

A second portico in front of the library takes advantage of the winter afternoon sun by creating a space sheltered from the wind.

The building is constructed of brick, with reinfroced concrete for the portico and some masonry walls of local stone. The sliding partitions are of wood.

The south facade has canvas awnings for the summer. A masonry wall encloses the service courtyard and the service area on the south facade, unifying the twin volumes of the main building and the garage.

Plans and view of the exterior

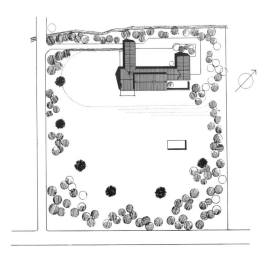

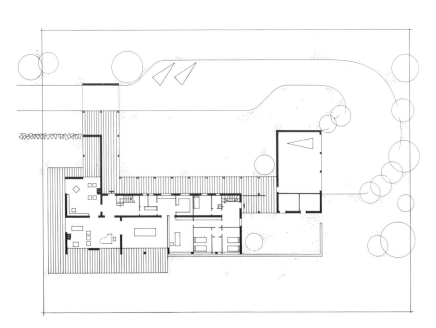

Private house

Antonio Bonet, architect
Golft residential development, Puigcerdà, Girona, 1967

In this, my frist encounter with a landscape of mountains and snow, I decided to use a kind of material which was completely new to me: an abundance of wood, slaty stone, and slate for the roofs.

In residential develpments such as this one, the propietors usually want the construction of their house to be treated as something personal, quite independent from the rest of the development, and the overall harmony of the complex tends to suffer from the negative consequences of this decision.

This does not happen, however, in small fishing or mountain villages, whose beauty and harmonious unity with the landscape are so much admired. Builders in these villages adopt elementary models which they then simply reproduce. In Puigcerdà, I decided to follow this wise course. Accordingly, all of the houses are based on one of four different models, with a single aesthetic constant. The first house type is one-storey and very extended; the second type, also single-storey, takes advantage of the slope of the roofs; the third type is two-storey and follows the gradient of the site, and the fourth type is semi-detached.

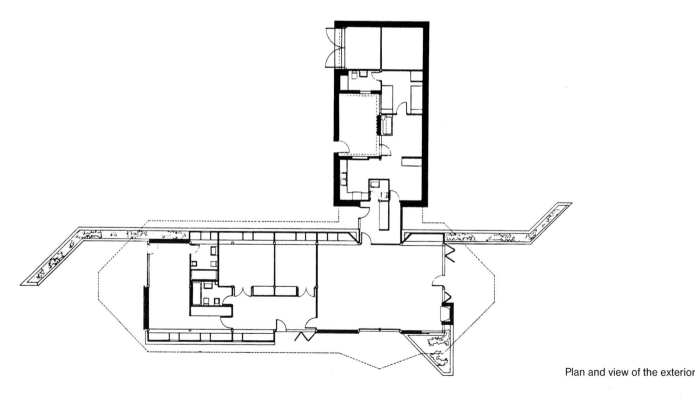

Plan and view of the exterior

44

Various views of the exterior, the
portico and detail of the interior

Various views and details of the
interior

49

Ajenjo house

Pere Llimona/Xavier Ruiz i Vallés, architects
Alp, Girona, 1965-1966

This group of constructions in the midst of the Cerdanya plain has been kept low so as to merge better with the surrounding fields.
In addition to the main house, there is a studio, a porters' lodge and a tool shed.

All of the buildings have white walls, with four-sided pitched roofs of slate over a wooden structure. All are single-storey so as not to project up more than is necessary.

The house is square in plan, with a central coutyard sheltered to the north. The studio, the children's house, is a minimal square space.

No attempt has been made to lay out a garden, beyond installing a swimming pool and planting a number of trees.

Plans, elevations and views of the exterior

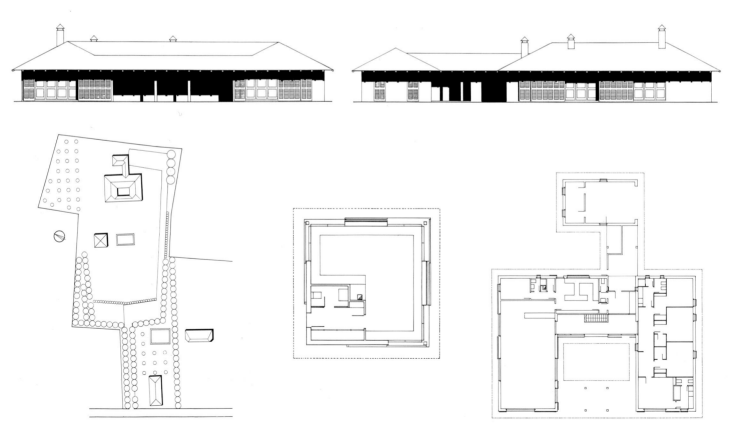

Robert house

Gabriel Robert, architect
Prullans, Lleida, 1977-1978

The backbone of the planning of this project consisted of the following premises:

1. Scrupulous respect for the meadow in which the house was to stand.
2. The incorporation into the project, as a principal element, of the exceptional views of the Segre valley and the Cadi mountain range.
3. The creation of a small urban-style layout linking the buildings to each other and to the town's road network.

On the basis of these premises, all of the existing trees (living and dead) were retained, siting the building in such a way as to respect both its privacy and its views of the countryside.

The most important elements, which ought to be noted, are:

– the manifest intention of expressing the various internal functions of the buildings on its exterior.
– the formalisation of the windows conditioned entirely by the wonderful views.
– the treatment of colour, aimed at clarifying the different levels of the house.

Plans, elevations, sections and views of the exterior

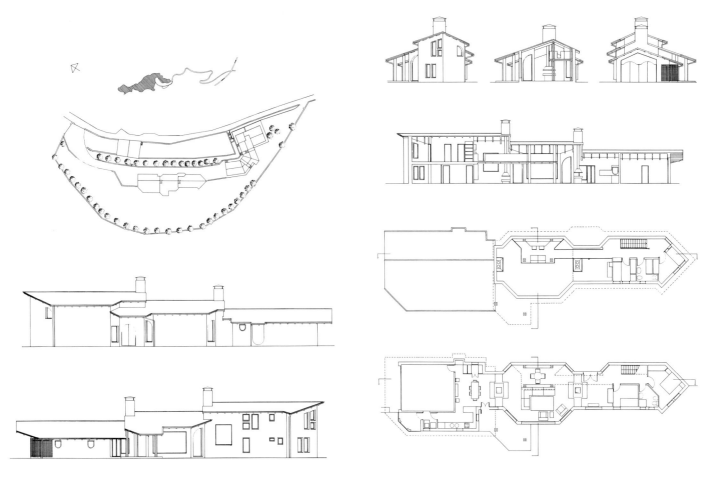

56

57

Various views of the interior

Various partial views of the exterior

Curtis house

Pere Aixas, Joan Ardévol, Sergi Godia,
Juli Laviña, Pep Urgell, estudi MAD
Auvinyà, Sant Julià de Lòria, Andorra, 1975-1978

This is an annexe to an existing chalet built of local stone and partly hidden by vegetation. It was designed as a very simple volume, with a flat roof to be covered by vegetation. The programme was developed on two levels: the ground floor for use as a garage, and the first floor, intended to function as a dwelling, independent from and complementary to the main house. The "real" facade of the annexe is set back from the road, and the wall here is differentiated from the rest of the volume to which it belongs.

The materials used are those traditional in constructions in the high mountains: stone and dovetailed wood.

Plans, section and view of the exterior

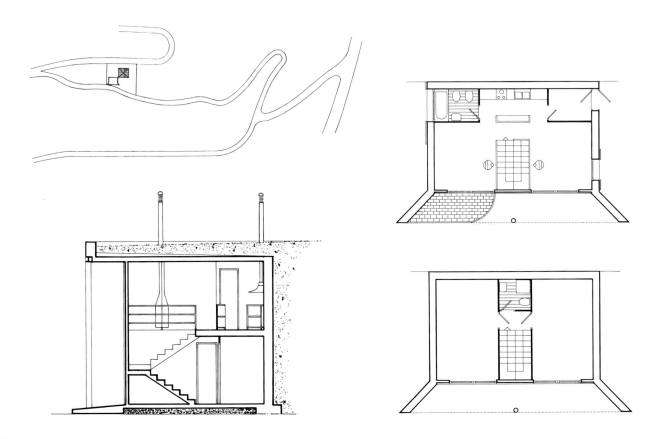

Details of the interior

Cal Nap

Cristian Cirici, architect
Queralbs, Girona, 1971-1972

Queralbs is a village in the Pyrinees situated about halfway up the side of Puigmal (at a height of between 1100 and 1200 metres approximately).

The house which we half reconstructed, half refurbished, had been used to keep livestock and fodder. It stands in the upper part of the village, near the Romanesque church.

We rebuilt the entire exterior volume fairly faithfully; the stone walls and slate roof are even of the same height, and have the same slope, as the original construction, since this was quite satisfactory. We changed the rest, because of its poor condition and because we wanted to lower the ceilings, with glazed openings in the roof through which to see the stars and the mountain peaks; we widened the stairs, painted the walls and the beams white, and made a number of other changes.

Plans, section and view of the access

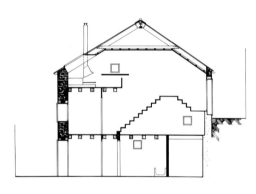

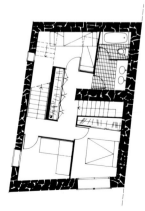
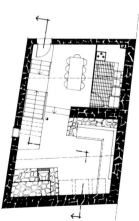

68

Various views and details of the
interior

Juvany house

Joan Rodon, architect
Areu, Lleida, 1989-1990

This is a private house built on the southeast corner of the church square in Areu. The basement and all of the ground floor, to be used as a garage, are independent of the rest of the house. An external staircase on the south facade leads up to the first floor, which contains the house's communal rooms.

The scheme for the Juvany house set out to integrate a new building into the established fabric of a rural village. The reduced dimensions and anarchic geometry of the plot suggested the construction of a single volume consisting of a rotated plane, without arrises, beneath a roof with deep eaves which dominates and orders the whole. The handrail of the external staircase forms a second plane which takes up the width of the eaves and attaches itself to the main volume, thus defining a sheltered space beneath the roof which is also occupied by the balcony off the bedrooms.

The two major openings in the house, the large living room window and the garage door have been effected by completely cutting through the wall, leaving the stone mass of the wall and the planes of the roof flags as the principal elements in the project.

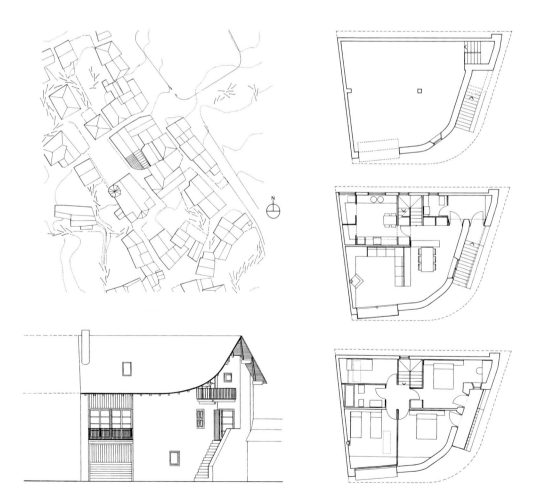

Plans, elevation and view of the exterior

Various views and details of the
exterior

Borda d'en Roy

Cristian Cirici, architect
Arrós, Vall d'Aran, Lleida, 1988-1990

This second residence was, until the beginning of 1988, a free-standing, two-storey construction. The upper floor was used as a hayloft, and the lower floor to keep cattle over the winter.

The basic intention orienting the whole refurbishment scheme was to conserve as far as possible all the elements which were in a good state of repair and which now constitute the outer skin of the building.

The only access to the building is the original entrance through the courtyard. From this partly roofed courtyard two separate doors lead into the house.

The cylindrical pillars and I-beams, of laminated steel, have all been left exposed. The floor and roof structures are of reinforced concrete, constructed using corrugated shuttering, painted white and left exposed to view.

Plans, section and view of the exterior

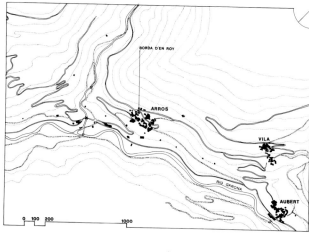

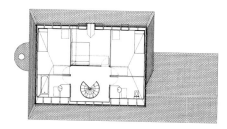

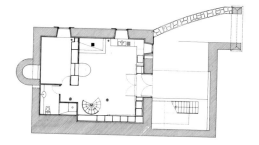

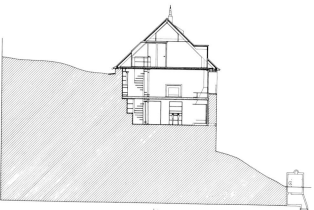

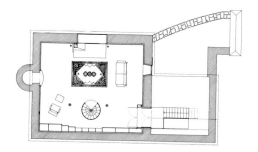

80

Various views and details of the
exterior and interior

Ca l'Agustí

Xavier Güell, architect
Arcavell, Lleida, 1987-1989

This house, situated in the upper part of the village, very close to the border with neighbouring Andorra, was the subject of a fairly sweeping internal reorganisation. In applying the programme for a second residence for a family of four, the original levels of the house were first changed in order to adapt them to a use more in keeping with the functional programme, and secondly, the existing openings in the facades were adapted to conform to the new interior distribution, in addition to the necessary creation of new windows to provide the users with more light and better views.

The north-facing part of the house has been treated as a single space giving onto o roofed terrace. Here we have the juxtaposition of two structures: one, more in line with the setting, in wood, and the other, more ordinary in treatment, at right angles to the first.

Plans, sections and view of the exterior

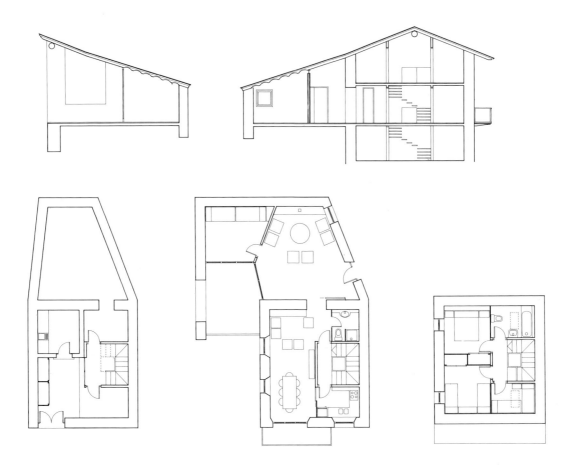

Various views of the interior

Various details of the exterior and interior

El Paller

Guillem Sáez, architect
Barruera, Vall de Boí, Lleida, 1970-1971

El Paller was originally designed and built as a second residence for its architect. The programme of requirements was therefore carried out in line with his family circumstances: kitchen-dining room-living room, small wine cellar, separate living room with fireplace, roofed terrace overlooking the garden, wood store, three double bedrooms and two bathrooms. All of this was accomodated in the former hayloft (*paller* in Catalan, hence the name) of the ruined house he had bought.

Given the reduced dimensions at the architect's disposal, the solution adopted integrates all of the necessary spaces by means of a projecting exterior staircase, which serves to articulate and interconnect all the different parts of the house.

The construction techniques and materials are those traditional to the area: masonry walls, dovetailed wooden floor, with wooden beams and a thermally insulated roof covered with slate.

The orientation of the window openings is calculated to ensure the best views of the surrounding landscape.

Plans, elevations and view of the exterior

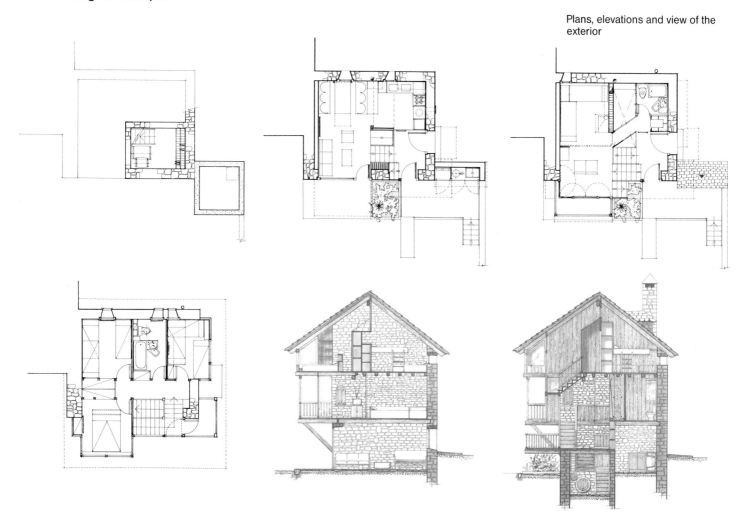

90

Various details and partial views of
the exterior and interior

Folgosa house

Francisco Javier Aguilar, Juan José Albors,
José Luis Canosa, architects
Arrós, Vall d'Aran, Lleida, 1973-1974

The house is land out in accordance with the terraces which shape the hillside in such a way that the stepping up of the different existing levels accomodates the placing of the various elements which make up the programme.

A staircase aligned with the longitudinal axis gives access to each of the platforms, establishing the sequence of entrance hall, living areas, dining room and kitchen, with the studio and bedrooms on the upper terraces.

The project thus sets out to accomodate itself to the gradient of the site and the form in which it is organised, providing the slope with a communicative sequence which runs through the house and gives access to the outdoor terraces, accordingly allows a view of the hillside beyond the house.

The building is roofed in the most immediate manner, by means of a single inclined roof plane parallel to the slope of the terrain.

The materials used on the facade are typical of the area: the slate roof and stone walls are united by a band of concrete which crowns and ties together the whole construction.

The interior of the house has white walls and wood floors.

Plans, sections and view of the house and its surroundings

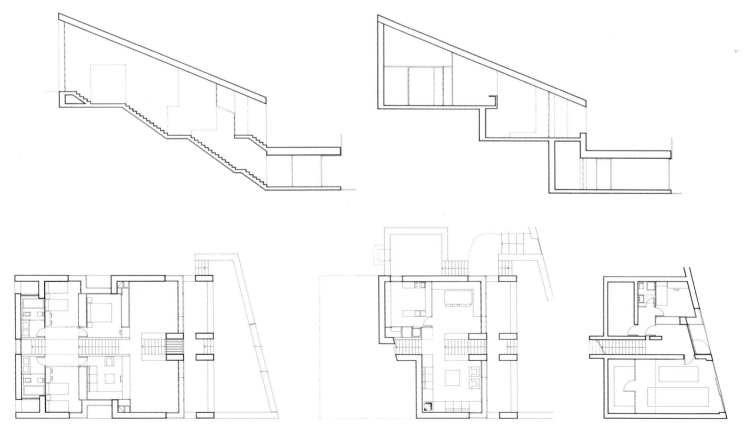

Font house

Miquel Espinet/Antoni Ubach, architects
Arcavell, Lleida 1988-1990

Arcavell, the last settlement before the border with Andorra, is the location for two intimately interconnected projects, both designed for the same family.

The first, in an old "borda" or cottage, 50 metres square, has been refurbished and converted for weekend use, and the second, standing in an adjacent meadow, is a wholly new building designed as a main residence for the family and their guests.

The complex is set down in the landscape as two superimpoed planes, horizontally enclosed and ordered by old masonry walls. The intervention in the "borda" is essentially interior.

The new building, on the other hand, a linear, single-storey development, presents a more complex insertion into the contours of the little village. The rigidity of the facade is relieved by the generous dimensions of the windows at the corners, and the systematic alignment of the rooms is complemented internally by a rich concentration space which is the centre of distribution for the whole house.

Plans, elevations, sections and view of the exterior

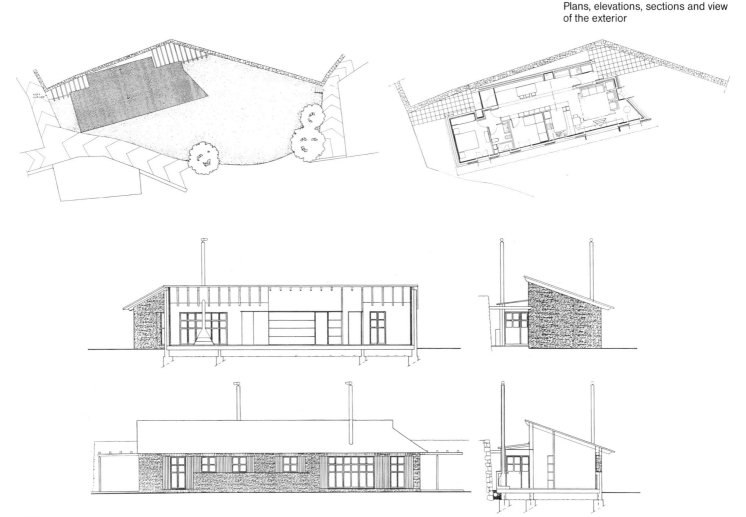

Previous pages: various interior
and exterior views of the house and
its surroundings

Various views and detaills
of the exterior and interior

Private house

Francisco Ribas, architect
Guils de Cerdanya, Girona, 1983-1985

This private house has been developed on the basis of an existing construction, the outer walls of which have been retained.

The plot, delimited by four streets in the centre of the little town of Guils, has a gentle north-south slope, with the building standing in the north-west corner, aligned with the streets.

The new construction is of sandstone, roofed with slate, in accordance with local building regulations.

The south facade (which enjoys sun and views) has been given large windows of toughened safety glass, basically in the living areas.

By contrast, the north facade, exposed to the cold wind from the Carol valley, has 40 × 40 cm openings, all the same, situated in accordance with the internal programme.

The majority of the openings in the original volume have been retained.

Plans, elevation and views of the exterior

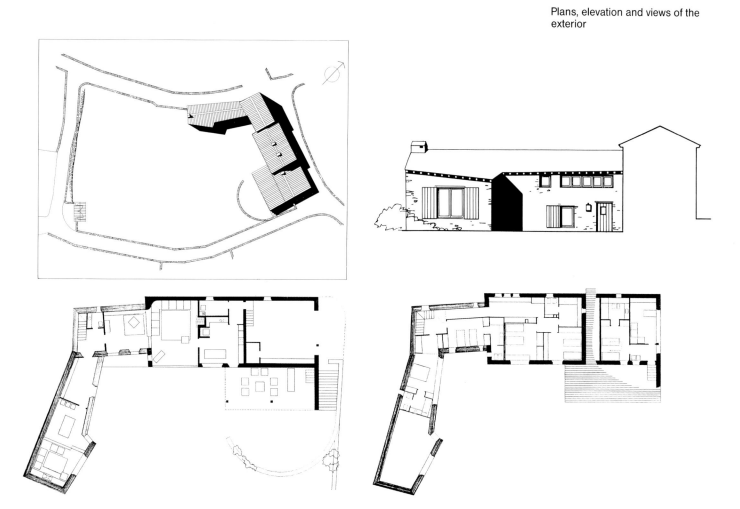

Various views and partial views of
the exterior and interior

Rius Fina house

Francesc Rius, architect
Bolvir, Girona, 1988-1990

The disposition of the plot, the longest side of which faces the best views and the optimum orientation, has been ably exploited in the construction of a building which is linear in plan, open to the south and closed to the north.

The house is organised by means of two volumes articulated by a closed portico which opens onto a small garden.

The two volumes are interconnected by the enclosed portico and the covered passageway which, together with the small portico to the east, form a transition space between exterior and interior.

These intermediary spaces between house and garden have been divided into two differently oriented areas in such a way that one space is sunny in winter and the other is shady in summer.

The aim was for the house to reap maximum benefit from the characteristics of the site and climate.

In the passageway and the portico, contact with the rock has been sought in order to take advantage of the heat of the earth as a regulating factor, preventing frezing in winter, when the house is uninhabited, and cooling the interior in summer.

Plan, elevation, section, construction detail and view of the house and its surroundings

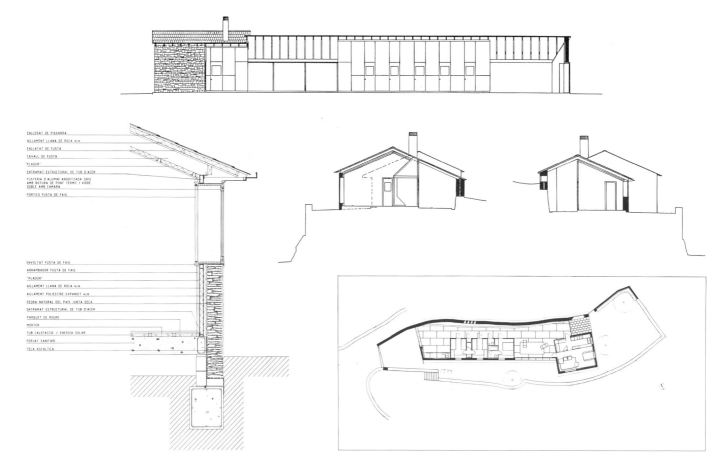

Various views and partial views of
the exterior

Various views of the interior and
detail of the facade

114

Sanmartí house

Jaume Sanmartí, architect
Prullans, Lleida, 1973-1975

The form of this house can be explained by the steep slope of the site on which it stands, and this is synthesised in the single plane of the roof, beneath which the programme of the private house is organised.

This programme is structured around a central reference space through which circulation pases, synthesising the whole house by means of its visual contact with the other rooms not spatially connected with it, with a functional autonomy of their own, such as the kitchen-dining room and the garage, which gives access to the house.

The slate-tiled roof, which follows the slope of the site, and the sandstone walls, rendered in dark brown stucco, allow the house to go almost unnoticed.

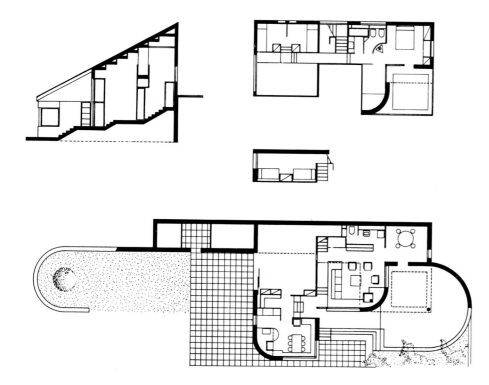

Plans, section and view of the
exterior

Following pages: various views of
the exterior and interior

Heredero house

Josep Martorell / Oriol Bohigas / David Mackay,
architects
Tredós, Vall d'Aran, Lleida, 1967-1968

This is a large house (479 m²) for summer and winter use belonging to a family with five children. It stands at an altitude of 1200 metres, near the Baqueira-Beret ski resort, overlooking the little village of Tredós, on a site with a pronouced south-westerly slope. The fundamental idea of the project was the ordering of four clearly physically differentiated environments laid out around a central nucleus which takes in the fireplaces, the services and the stairs. Each of these areas, with its own independent structure and services, interrelated only by spatially differentiated "bridges", can expand independently and in accordance with its own laws of growth, by way of axes which are expressed on the exterior in the gables of the slate roof and in the interior by the direction of the wooden lamellas of the ceiling. The house has been treated as an isolated, exceptional object, set down on the mountainside with the aim of coherently relating to the wildness of the landscape and the visual characteristics of the local traditional architecture. This image is reinforced by the succesion of of parallel stone walls that constitute a base which provides a certain visual stability.

Plans, axonometric sketch and view of the exterior of the house and its surroundings

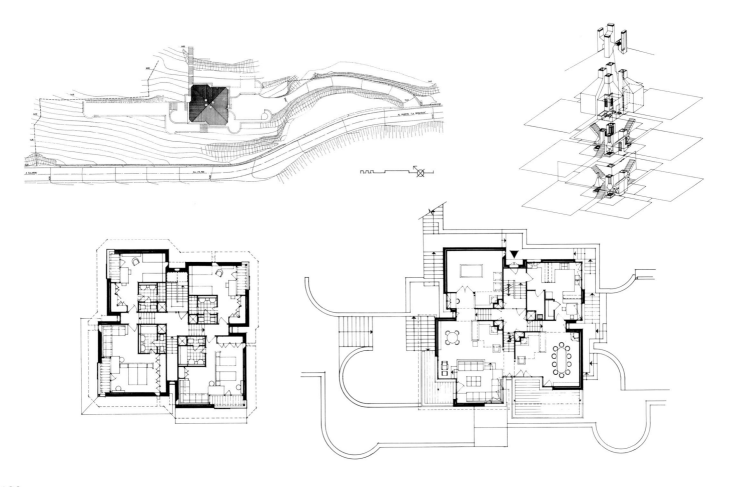

120

View of the exterior and detail of
one of the terraces

125

Martí Campanyà house

Josep Maria Sostres, architect
Ventolà, Girona, 1971

In this house, with its privileged position and exceptional views, particular importance has been given to the roofs.

The programme for this second residence is organised by means of the entrance axis, with the daytime area and the bedrooms laid out on either side of it.

The special attention given by the architect to local materials, while imposing his own contemporary interpretation on their formal design, is an important aspect of his far from prolific architectural output. The topography of the site, the surrounding country, and the harsh winter temperatures of a high mountain climate, as well as the local building tradition, have all, as the architect explains, influenced the character of the construction.

Plan, elevations, section and views of the exterior

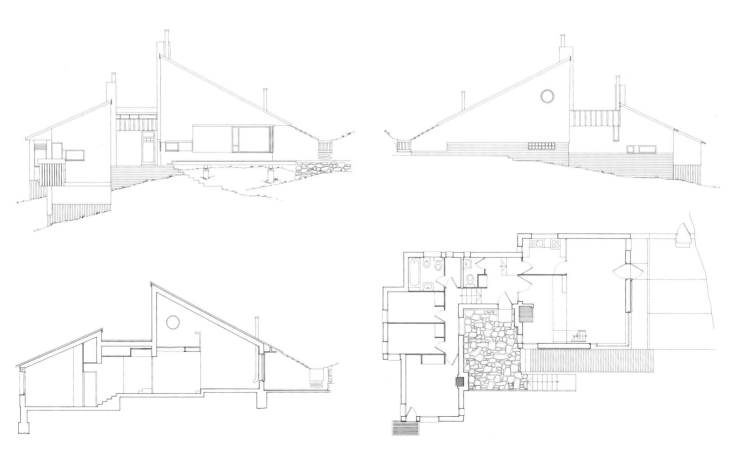

127

Various views and details of the
exterior and interior

Mateu Martínez house

Jaume Sanmartí, architect
Tartera, Alp, Girona, 1971-1972

The project for this house is a response to the demands made on the architecture of the lower Pyrinees in terms of climate and landscape, as distinct from the sociological and environmental commonplaces associated with a second residence.

Without paying undue attention to the conventional inclination towards a language in line with "tasteful" vernacular architecture, the house sits easily on its site, sheltering its interior and exterior spaces from the two winds which implacably dominate the valley. In consequence, its directs its gaze towards the peaks and ridges which bound the Cerdanya to north and south.

The overall from of the building and the materials employed in its construction are the result of previously established criteria, which have been applied naturally and effectively without falling into the clichés mentioned above.

It should be borne in mind that many of these premises were discussed and agreed with the client in advance, and that the quality of the results, and the satisfaction produced by contemplating the house today are the outcome of this dialogue and good relationship.

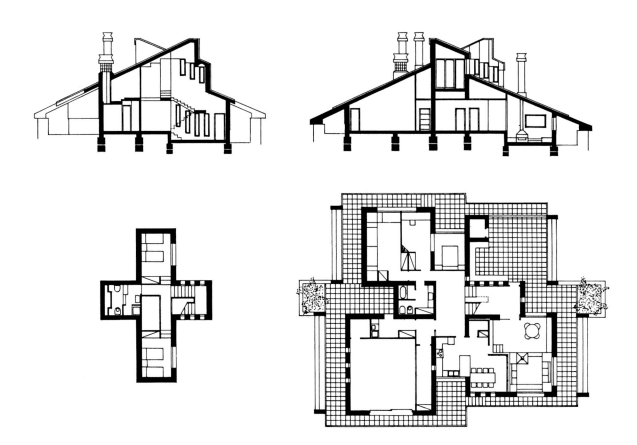

Various views of the interior and
detail of the exterior

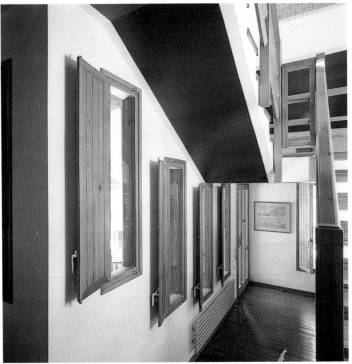

Mairal Ceresuela house

Paco Puyalto, architect
Gresa-Laspuña, Huesca, 1986-1988

The evolution of this project was largely conditioned by the physical characteristics of the site.

On the one hand, our building organises the space, and on the other, it has had to respect the elements which determine it. In the first place, the construction breaks up in an orderly fashion, occupying different zones and creating spaces of different characters over the sequence of terraces.

Secondly, the lower floor of the main building has been converted into yet another part of the base of existing stone. In this way, the upper floor, which moreover is not a solidly rounded volume, seems to rest on the masonry wall.

The natural change in level between the terraces or bands has prompted the particular organisation to be seen in the house. The area for nighttime use is located on the lower level, and the daytime area on the first floor. This has allowed a better visual and neighbourly relationship with the rest of the village, which extends to the north-east, as well as greater formal freedom in the design of the more representative spaces (entrance hall, living room-dining room).

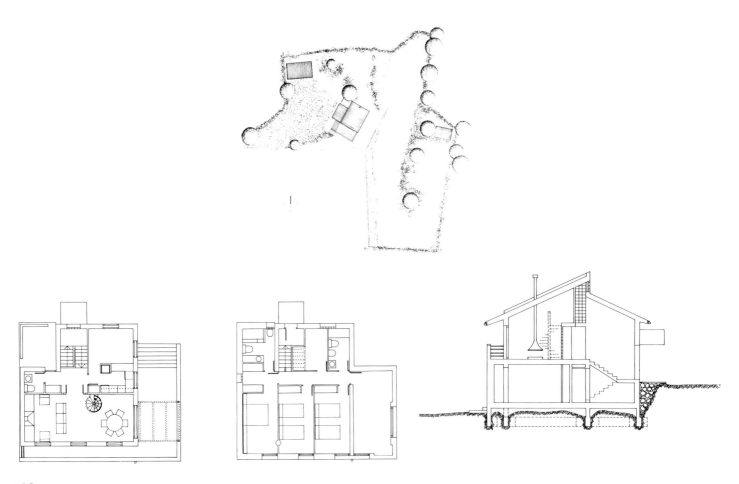

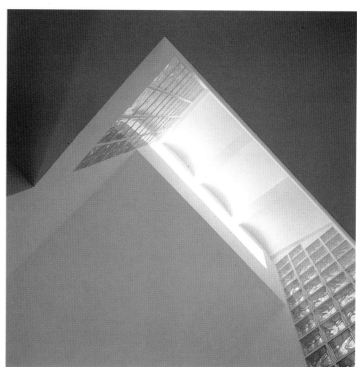

Various views of the exterior and interior

Xampeny house

Josep Maria Sostres, architect
Ventolà, Girona, 1971

This house is contemporary with the Martí Campanyà house and essentially follows the same distribution scheme, although with a controlled movement in the floor plan and roofs.

Sostres rotates the orthogonal layout of the plan forty-five degrees, leaving the rear roof, with its steeper inclination, to come to rest against the hillside.

The proper place for the fireplace in the living room is at the nerve centre of the entire space, which, with its different levels, lends itself to the various functions being carried on there.

The same repertoire of materials employed in both houses, their proximity, and the way that each confidently engages in a uniquely central role entitles them to particular attention, and allows them to be classed as exemplary.

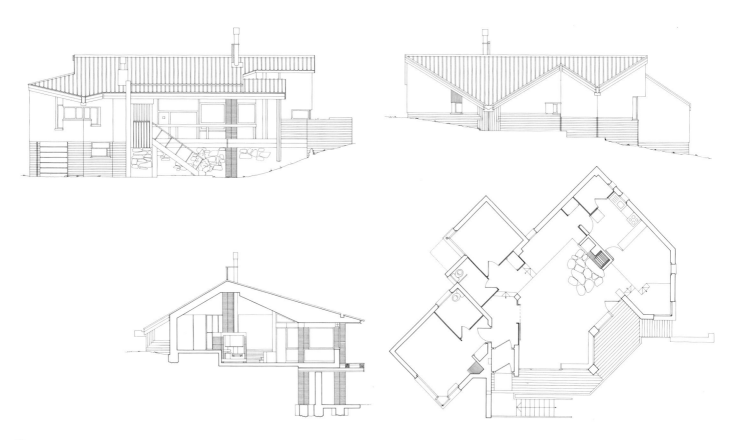

Plan, section, elevations and view of
the house and its surroundings

144